ANGELO M. SWINSON

Presented To: Ms. Roschonda Harris

Thanks 4 Everything

From:

Date March 15th 2013

NO MORE DYSFUNCTIONAL LOVE

ANGELO M. SWINSON

NO MORE DYSFUNCTIONAL LOVE

ANGELO SWINSON

Husbands love your wives, even as Christ also loved the church, and gave himself for it;

Ephesians 5:25

NO MORE DYSFUNCTIONAL LOVE

Swinson Legacy Publishing
Riverdale, GA 30296 * 404-997-1173
Email: angeloswinson36@gmail.com

© 2013 Angelo Swinson
ISBN:

Book Cover Design and Proofreading:
Ellis & Ellis Consulting Group, LLC
www.ellisandellisconsulting.org

Editing:
Aziza I. Robertson's Relations and Editing (A.I.R.R.E)
Public Relations & Editing
AIRREfirm@gmail.com

Additional Proofreading: Cindy Lockwood

Unless otherwise noted Scripture quotations are taken from: The Holy Bible, New King James Version, New Living Translation, and English Standard versions of the Bible. Some scripture quotations from Scripture contain words emphasized by the author. These words are not emphasized in the original bible version.
© 1979, 1980, and 1982 by Thomas Nelson, Inc.
Used by permission. ALL RIGHTS RESERVED.

No part of this publication may be reproduced, stored in a retrieval system, or transmitted, in any means electronic, mechanical, photocopying, recording, or otherwise without the prior written permission of the author.

Printed in United States of America

DEDICATION

To everyone who has encountered dysfunctional love. To my wife and queen: you are the complete opposite of what Dysfunctional Love is. This book could not have been written if it wasn't for your unexplainable love. Thank you for displaying what healthy love is. ...To my children Dontario, Angel, & Angelique: your dad wrote this book so that you can have something to help guide you and prevent you from encountering some of the dysfunction your dad and others have encountered. To my mother Lisa Mitchell and my father Michael Angelo Swinson: if it wasn't for God selecting the two of you, it would be impossible for me to talk about dysfunctional love. To the both of you, I thank you for your unconditional love. To my siblings Kandice Michael , Monique, Jazmynn and Zuri this is for you. To the rest of my family, near and far , thank you for the roles you have played in my life. Last but not least to the greatest church in the world, Servants

NO MORE DYSFUNCTIONAL LOVE

of Love! You've helped empower your pastor to empower others to not become dysfunctional in their love. I love you!

ANGELO M. SWINSON

ACKNOWLEDGEMENTS

I want to thank God for creating me with a purpose and anointing me to write this book. Without having a personal relationship with you Lord, none of this would have been possible. To Prophet Luther Mckinstry III, thank you for writing the foreword of my first book. It is truly a dream come true. I am humbled to have someone of your caliber endorse my first project, and am truly grateful and humbled unto God.

To everyone who helped answer my countless number of questions concerning my book: I appreciate you all very much. To Prophetess Cherylrese Barconia , Apostle De-borah Champion Elder Olivia Stith- Bynum and Minister Paul K. Ellis Jr., I decree special blessings over your life!

To everyone else who I may not have named that played a role in completing this book; to everyone that believed in me and gave me an endorsement book review and support : I am humbled that you have considered to be a blessing to me in that way. Apostle Eddrick & Pastor Faylonta High , Prophet Terrell Turner, Pastor Sonia Dolano, China Smith, Mr. Mike Strzempka, Jamena Spann, Bishop Robert Hunt, Apostles Denise & Samuel Chase, Pastor Paula Cooke , Vanda V. Wilson-Wormack, Dr. Uyi Abraham, Pastor Jason Rowland, & Kelly Cole . I speak bountiful blessings over all of your lives in Jesus name. We would like to personally acknowledge you and thank you for supporting the vision that God has given me and helping this dream become a reality.

Thanks you all for allowing Swinson Legacy to use some of your personal experiences to bring healing and restoration to many. The characters in this book are of those whom I know personally, including some of my personal experiences throughout the years, and I pray that this non-fictional book is life changing too many. I want to thank the clergy and non-clergy that shared some of their most personal experiences that helped steer this book in a life-changing direction.

ANGELO M. SWINSON
ENDORSEMENTS

"No More Dysfunctional Love Is A Book That Is Very Needed In The Kingdom, To Many Amazing People Are Settling For Dysfunctional Love, When They Could Have So Much More! Apply The Nuggets & Wisdom In This Book and I Promise You Won't Become One Of Them.

Kelly Cole
#1 Best Selling Author of Conversations With Sharks
CEO Prime Time Marketing

This book is an extreme eye opener, with exceptional personal testimonials, of finding out that special one for you. The details in Angelo's book, has obviously caused him to research information regarding preparation for that special one. I have never believed that God made choices for you, however he does show his approval or disapproval of the choices we make. This book seems to be a great start towards a wonderful future, for those that are searching for destiny partners.

Prophet Terrell Turner
Word in Motion Ministries

NO MORE DYSFUNCTIONAL LOVE

The connection my wife and I had when we first met was so powerful from the first day, something I never experienced with anyone else. I knew God had sent her to me because she had all the qualities I desired in a woman. We discovered early on that prayer and meditation were the only answers for some of our toughest struggles. This is something we still practice daily. Our deep faith in the Lord and commitment to each other has kept our relationship growing through the first seven years. Realizing it is not without hard work and dedication, we are looking forward to our family's lifetime together. Your book serves as an inspiration and confirmation that the bond between a married couple is well worth the effort.

China Smith Heavy Weight Champ China Smith
Director of Manatee PAL Boxing & Fitness
TEAM CHINA SMITH

ANGELO M. SWINSON

Powerful, spirit driven and to the point are a few words that come to mind as I read, " No Dysfunctional Love" by Prophet Angelo Swinson. The Lord has empowered his spokesman to bring a fresh word and teaching on kingdom unions between a man and woman to the forefront for others to learn. I'm sure when one finishes reading this book, they will have a greater incite on the spiritual and natural relationships that God has predestined for them.

Elder Olivia Stith-Bynum
Author of, "If God Is My Lover, Why Is My Bed So Cold?"
"Lord Is Boaz Lost? Or Am I Just in the Wrong Field?"

NO MORE DYSFUNCTIONAL LOVE

A must read....

I believe that this book is not only "timely" but is also "long awaited". Divinely inspired of the Lord as communicated to His writer, for such a time as now". Not failing to add "for future generations to come". Again, "long awaited" and "expectedly welcome". It is not only "eye opening" to the reader, confirming that God has 'great purpose' in His intents of joining 2 person's to "oneness" but it also inspiring in many ways as to the importance of "God's hand selection" of that "one". The way that Pastor Angelo Swinson unveils the process to preparation, his own personal experience, as well as sharing the experiences of others is to be greatly admired and welcomed with "much enthusiasm". I am blessed without measure by what I have read up to date, speaking to me "personally" in my own quest for the "one", the "one" that only God Himself has been preparing for such a time and a season as only He has.

God richly bless, you "the reader", Pastor Swinson "God's anointed writer" and most importantly "the prosperity of this book, No more Dysfunctional Love"

Pastor Sonia Dalano
Tampa, FL

"It is my belief that the second most important thing a person will do in their life, after giving their life to Christ, is deciding with whom they will spend their life with in a marriage relationship. "No More Dysfunctional Love" addresses this point quite thoroughly. This book is a must-read for God's daughters who are yet "waiting for," "The One."

Vanda V. Wilson-Wormack,
CEO & Founder
ePastorsNetwork.com

NO MORE DYSFUNCTIONAL LOVE

No More Dysfunctional love is a great easy read. This book is filled with divine insights that will help the reader to know how to spot the "right one" that God has for them and how to experience real love in the marriage. You will be empowered to discover your true identity in Christ that will prepare you for real love. Prophet Angelo Swinson is a major voice in this generation, and this book is destined to be a success.

Dr. Uyi Abraham
President, Higher Place Christian University
Senior Pastor, Elevate Church

The body of Christ has undoubtedly seen a misrepresentation of "love" over the past few decades. As the word declares, men have become lovers of themselves, thus we have and are passing on a twisted version of love to this generation. Divorce is ramped. Man no longer marries for love - but for lust. What are we to do? How can we rekindle the agape love as in the days of old? In his powerful and insightful book, "No More Dysfunctional Love", Angelo Swinson captures the heart and essence of the change needed in this hour. He profoundly exposes the curse placed on genuine pure love and teaches us how we can all experience the love intended before the foundation of the world. As you read this thought-provoking book and listen to various accounts of real-life stories, your heart will be pricked to change and share. Swinson uniquely serves as the pencil God needed to document his plans for this "crazy thing called love!"

Paul K. Ellis Jr.
CEO
Ellis & Ellis Consulting Group, LLC.
Author – "Shifting a Generation"

NO MORE DYSFUNCTIONAL LOVE

Pastor/Prophet Swinson, a fellow kingdom laborer where we lead in the same city where single individuals way outnumber married couples, inspires believers through this masterpiece in finding the "One" for their life that "The One" has ordained and destined. This work will encourage the reader to arrest the enemy of dysfunctional love and run toward their divine prince or princess.

Jason Rowland

Living Waters Atlanta

livingwaters.tv

I'd have to say my favorite three chapters were Overcoming Past Hurts, Waiting on the One, and After the Turbulence. Even in that they are all great chapters and this book possess the ability to bless those who are open to receive what is birthed in this book. The couple examples flowed really well with the theme of each chapter. I will certainly purchase this book when it comes out. It's much needed in the Kingdom of God.

Cindy S. Lockwood

ANGELO M. SWINSON

TABLE OF CONTENTS

	Foreword	18
	Preface	20
Chapter 1	What is Dysfunction?	23
Chapter 2	Overcoming Past Hurts	36
Chapter 3	Not Giving into Temptation	46
Chapter 4	After the Turbulence	59
Chapter 5	Waiting on the One	72
Chapter 6	Inspite of Unconditional Love	86
Chapter 7	The Advice	97
Chapter 8	Putting God first	114
Chapter 9	What are the Singles Saying?	125
About the Author		142

NO MORE DYSFUNCTIONAL LOVE
FOREWORD

This book is a must read for anyone who is serious about understanding the importance of divine connections. As you read this book, I admonish you not to just simply read the pages but rather to allow the pages to read you. Do not be afraid to open up your heart and allow these God-ordained words to assimilate and integrate into the fabric of your life! To many people in the Body of Christ are out of the will of God because they did not wait on God to reveal to them who the right ONE was for their life. To many of us operated out of emotion instead of hearing the voice of the Father.

Angelo Swinson is uniquely anointed for this task because he is not afraid to share the disappointments and hardships that he experienced on this journey, which serves as valuable tools as we sojourn through life. In addition, the various testimonies only help ignite the flame needed to be alert and watchful for the adversary. It is not a surprise that the Holy Spirit would download this valuable information to Angelo because he has been prepared for such a time as this to teach, impart, and share from the tables of his heart and prepare us as we wait for THE ONE!

Be prepared to be confronted, challenged, and ultimately TRANSFORMED!

Prophet Luther McKinstry, III
Luther Mckinstry Ministries
www.luthermckinstryministries.org/

NO MORE DYSFUNCTIONAL LOVE
PREFACE

This book is designed to help strengthen relationships and marriages that are on a downward spiral. The purpose of this book is to help bring clarity and understanding to what love is through transparency and honesty, and expound on the purpose of love. This book is designed to help those who to need solutions and answers on how to overcome dysfunctional issues. The goal is to reach many with strategies and principles on how to survive any season of turbulence.

Romans 8:28
And we know that God causes everything to work together for the good of those who love God and are called according to his purpose for them.

Are you tired of having dysfunctional relationships? Are you are looking for direction on how to survive dysfunctional relationships? This book displays the purpose of dysfunction. I have realized many of us have seen dysfunction and have experienced it, but many of us have not shared what it is that helped them through. It is not until you recognize the dysfunction, that you are willing to make a change. I decree that there is still hope for your marriage! This book will show you how to take a stand for righteousness and learn how to love and experience the ultimate reward of forgiveness. If I can cheer somebody with a word or song, if I can show somebody he is traveling wrong, then my living shall not be in vain. *If I Can Help Somebody*. A. Bazel Androzzo, © 1945, Alma B. Androzzo

This book attacks dysfunctional issues head-on while sharing kingdom principles and strategies to defeat it. Dysfunction can happen before and after marriage, and it is important to understand the protocol on how to deal with these issues. I know that many of us have seen dysfunction or have been raised in dysfunction, but don't know how to come out of dysfunction. It is not until we have a mindset change or healing that takes place that we move forward. I have personal experiences and a few experiences of other married couples centered on dysfunctional topics, what we went through, how we overcame it, and how things got better.

This book was birthed out of a dysfunctional relationship our son was going through. It is to help those who are looking to be married and help those who are already married to have a prosperous marriage and relationship.

Philippians 4:13
I can do all things through Christ who strengthens me.

… ANGELO M. SWINSON

CHAPTER ONE
WHAT IS DYSFUNCTION?

"Soul-mates are people who bring out the best in you. They are not perfect but are always perfect for you."
- ***Author Unknown***

Many would say anything that is not the Cosby family is dysfunction. The Cosby family was on a television show call the Cosby show. This consisted of a husband and wife and four children. This television show aired from the mid 1980s to the early 1990s. They displayed a healthy well-balanced family with both parents at home. Perhaps some of us didn't watch the Cosby show, but we may be familiar with the TV show the Brady bunch.

The Brady bunch was a popular television show that aired in the late 1960's to the mid 1970s. This was a story in which two families merged together to make one happy family. If you didn't have this at home then you were considered dysfunctional, broken, or even label as being a child out of wedlock. For example some men and women react and act certain ways because of what was missing in their life. Some of them lacked the proper attention they needed, which has brought forth a behavior in which they perceive attention to be.

It was never the purpose of God for families to be broken or dysfunctional. However, He will use those very things for His glory by showing others than even in your dysfunction it is for my glory. The scripture that comes to mind is

Romans 8:28

"And we know that all things work together for good to them that love God, to them who are the called according to his purpose".

Dysfunction means abnormality or impairment in the function of a specified bodily organ or system. We must first realize where the dysfunction came from and then work toward a solution of how to overcome dysfunction. I am a firm believer that dysfunction can be a seed that is planted in us. The word seed means a flowering plant's unit of reproduction, capable of developing into another such plant. This seed can be planted in us when we were young or throughout the years. Whenever a seed begins to grow it then takes on roots that are deep in the soil. It's not until you realize that you don't have to be dysfunctional that you work on not allowing yourself to be that way. There are many different ways that a person can become dysfunctional.

For example some of us have experienced mental, physical, emotional, or even spiritual abuse throughout the years. Some of us didn't receive the proper love or attention that we needed and this has caused you to be dysfunctional. I want to inform you that you can be better than those who were dysfunctional to you .I believe that many of us have to look at dysfunction in the right way. The hold of Dysfunction should be something that drives us not dries us. By channeling more positive energy instead of negative energy, we will begin to see more change based off of positive

NO MORE DYSFUNCTIONAL LOVE

reinforcement. Reinforcement means the process of encouraging or establishing a belief or pattern of behavior.

Dysfunction is something that some of us are accustomed to primarily because of what we have seen others do. For instance, some of us come from broken homes in which our parents were dysfunctional. This type of behavior can continue to grow if we allow ourselves to follow the same patterns of others. I would like to say that just because someone else acts this way around you doesn't mean that is the way you have to be. Even though everyone you know is dysfunctional, this doesn't mean that you will be dysfunctional.

You don't have to be a product of the environments that you have been associated with. The word product means a substance produced during a natural, chemical, or manufacturing process. We have to develop a mindset that I dare to be different. Notice whenever you see a commercial about the army they always mention be all that you can be. I want to tell the person that is reading this chapter be all you can. Don't limit yourself to where you are right now.

Never be afraid to step out into the unfamiliar and the first to do something. You may be the very person that brings your family out of poverty. You may be the very first person to cause your family to further their education. I have something that I always say to myself when I look at goal setting. We always have heard this saying *"The Sky is Limit".* I say to myself I don't want to just reach the sky because that is a limit.

I want to reach beyond the sky and go beyond my expectation. The word limit means a point or level beyond which something does not or may not extend or pass. We must realize that we were not put here just for ourselves but there is someone else that will be impacted by our choices and decisions. Please remember this popular saying, what you do today will affect how things will unfold tomorrow. Fathers and Mothers what you are doing to make an influence in your children's lives. The scripture tells us in

Proverbs 13:22
A good man leaves an inheritance to his children's children: and the wealth of the sinner is laid up for the just.

We are to be trendsetters and trailblazers for others that will come behind.

We are the creation of God and He doesn't look at us the way that man looks at us. The scripture tells us in

Psalm 139:14
I will praise thee; for I am fearfully and wonderfully made: marvelous are thy works; and that my soul knoweth right well.

Once you identify and see how God made you, you will see yourself the way that God sees you. It's not until you began speaking good things over your life and not negative things that you will began to change. We must look at ourselves and say this is where I came from but that is not what I am going to be. We should look at ourselves and say this where I am now but this not where I will end up. The scripture tells us in

Jeremiah 29:11

*For I know the thoughts that I think toward you, saith the L*ORD*, thoughts of peace, and not of evil, to give you an expected end.*

The word expected means Regard (something) as likely to happen. This is an indication God desires for you to be blessed and experience his abundance. However there is a process in which we have to go through in order to enjoy His promises. Some of us experience different trials than other but it is important to keep in mind that what doesn't kill you makes you stronger. Always remember that whenever you encounter struggles and setbacks that God has spoken a word over your life for you to have an expected end.

NO MORE DYSFUNCTIONAL LOVE

There is a difference from expecting and wanting something. Wanting something means not existing or supplied; absent. To want means that it is not given but expected means you it shall be given. The scripture says in

John 10:10

The thief cometh not, but for to steal, and to kill, and to destroy: I am come that they might have life, and that they might have it more abundantly.

I would like to pause for a moment and have you recite this prayer with me. I do understand that normally prayer is given at the beginning or the end … However it is important that we allow ourselves to be sensitive to the needs others … I believe that the words that are about to be released are going to break every chain and cycle off of your life. Now it's time to position yourself to be freed from the mindset of dysfunction.

Father God in the name of Jesus I ask that you help me in this state of brokenness. God I ask that you help me through this struggle and cycle in my life. Father I need direction, I need clarity, I need the wisdom and the insight on how to become better. God I ask that not my will but your will be done. God I surrender every mindset and agenda that I set for myself and I am open to receive a deposit from you concerning my life. Father God I thank you in advance for allowing me to release and surrender every weight and all the pressure of yesterday. I ask that you help me look at a life in a new way and that you fill me with your spirit. Help me remove any hindrances that are in my life so I can embrace and receive my new beginning in Jesus name I pray....

Now allow me to introduce you to a couple by the name of Lynette and Bobby. Lynette and Bobby were set up on a blind date by two of their friends. Lynette and Bobby began dating for nine months after the blind date they went on. Now they have they have been married for 16 years since they got married. Lynette and Bobby got married without receiving any guidance or spiritual advice.

NO MORE DYSFUNCTIONAL LOVE

Lynette and Bobby didn't receive any counseling on any premarital topics .Which could have prevented some of the dysfunction that we shall discuss later on. This couple didn't get the opportunity to discuss their views separately before saying they do. Lynette and Bobby encountered a lot of hardship in their relationship and marriage because of lack of wise counsel. For example they had to walk out a process in which they wish they didn't have to go through.

They then realized that their marriage was something that was sacred unto God and they didn't want to give up due to the dysfunction. Lynette and Bobby do have love for each other but the dysfunction has caused a strain on their relationship over the years. Some of the ways that they have learned to overcome the dysfunction is lay everything out on the table. Communication during dysfunction can prevent other dysfunction. They have learned that it is important to talk things out and find solutions to fix the dysfunction.

Lynette and Bobby have realized that holding it in is not best way to handle dysfunction. The reason why many couples are dysfunctional is because of what they are lacking. Some of us are unable to effectively communicate with one another causing dysfunction. Lack of communication causes the restoration process to be stagnating. The word stagnate means to cease developing; become inactive or dull.

Lynette and Bobby believe that it is very important to know what you want in a marriage before you say I do. It is very important to get to know that person before you jump the broom. Some things can be prevented later if more things are discussed early on in relationships.

I have discovered that whenever marriages are dysfunctional, it is because there is lack somewhere in the marriage. You have existed in the marriage but you are not living.

You haven't been able to grow with one another and allow you all to learn each other's differences. I believe that the reason why some of

NO MORE DYSFUNCTIONAL LOVE

us are dysfunctional is because of what we have experienced in past relationships. Lynette and Bobby believe that everyone has weaknesses and shouldn't allow the opinions of others to cause you in stay in the state of dysfunction. Whenever you stay in a place of dysfunction then the fruit can come forth in the marriage.

If you can remember these few simple principles you will never have to be concerned about being dysfunctional any longer. You must remember to change your mindset and want better for yourself than what you have now. It is important to dare to be different no matter what it looks like you will be determined to be successful. Remember that you are not a product of where you come from just because you are from there. I hear all the time how people say they are from this city and that city.

You can be the voice of influence in your community, neighborhood, school, and church or wherever life's path takes you. The scripture tells us in

Romans 12:2

And be not conformed to this world: but be ye transformed by the renewing of your mind, that ye may prove what is that good, and acceptable, and perfect, will of God.

The scripture tells us in

2 Corinthians 5:17

Therefore if any man be in Christ, he is a new creation: old things are passed away; behold, all things are become new.

That means that you were dysfunctional which is past tense and you are now functional which is present. The difference between your past and your present is this: One of them you used to be and one of them is what you are now.

"A true friend knows your weaknesses but shows you your strengths; feels your fears but fortifies your faith; sees your anxieties but frees your spirit; recognizes your disabilities but emphasizes your possibilities."

- *William Arthur Ward*

NO MORE DYSFUNCTIONAL LOVE
CHAPTER TWO

OVERCOMING PAST HURTS

Written by Shantel Swinson

"Keep in mind that the true measure of an individual is how he treats a person who can do him absolutely no good." - ***Ann Landers***

It is very important to overcome past hurts because if not it can hinder your future. The word-overcome means succeed in dealing with (a problem or difficulty). A lot of us have not dealt with our past and it causes those in our future to pay for someone else's mistake .It is very important to be healed emotionally so that we can enjoy our blessings. Now allow me to introduce a couple to you by the name of Liz and Jim.

Liz and Jim met on Christmas in 1992 at Jim's mother's house. They dated for about 6 months and got married in June of 1992. They have married for two decades during which they both have had much they have overcome since then. For instance Liz and Jim come from two different types of backgrounds. They both have different life experiences that required them to heal from their past issues. It is very important to be healed from the heartbreak of past relationships. This may include mistrust, unforgiveness, anger, bitterness, and resentment. Before they got married they didn't know they both needed healing.

They began praying and seeking God for His will to be done in their marriage. Through this process God revealed to them the root of their issues concerning their lives. God revealed where the hindrance was coming from, which was what was preventing them for walking in the purpose God had for their lives. Jim had to be freed from the control of his family. This was a being hindrance in their marriage.

Through the Holy Spirit that we were able to recognize, repent and be delivered from those strongholds. It is important to forgive your past in order for your relationship to be whole, loving and fulfilled. They have learned how to accept, respect and love each other for who they are. They have not started to celebrate and reverence who God made them and minister to each other on every level. They are still learning and growing together to this very day. They have been married 19 years.

Some of the other reasons why it is important to let go of past hurt is because God cannot fulfill His purpose in your life until you are healed. It prevents the relationship of full commitment and satisfaction. It can destroy you and those you are connected to. Unforgiveness is a device for the enemy to show up whenever he wants and take complete control of your relationship. The most important key to dealing with past hurts is to face them.

You cannot overcome what you are not willing to face. You have to be honest and upfront about what has hurt you. As women you are taught it is better to be seen then to be heard, nobody like a loud, loose mouth woman so you tend to bottle stuff and just smile and say "I'm okay" when in reality everything on the inside is screaming help! As men you tend to hear "A man is suppose to be hard and don't show any emotions" so what instead of dealing with the thing that caused you pain some find ways of releasing by drinking, smoking or womanizing all to pacifier the pain instead of facing it.

1 Samuel 17:26

And David spake to the men that stood by him, saying, What shall be done to the man that killeth this Philistine, and taketh away the reproach from Israel? For who is this uncircumcised Philistine, that he should defy the armies of the living God?

In 1 Samuel David was faced with a dilemma; here was Goliath (the giant) that went about terrorizing the people of God and because everyone was so afraid of this giant no one would face him because here he was this 9 foot 6 inch monster that could just crash you with one blow. And David spoke out "who is this uncircumcised Philistine"? Though these hurts may be huge and it seems like they will just crash you at the thought of them, you cannot be delivered from what you are afraid to face. No matter how big, tall or small the hurt is you have to make up in your mind today is the day I will face this giant and cut off its head. The longer you suppress it, cover it up or bottle it up the more it grows and hinders you and stagnates you and prevents you from walking in totally obedience and happiness.

Dealing with past Hurt Exercise:

Take a piece of paper and a pen; sit down in a quiet place where you can think without distractions or interruptions. Begin to think back to everything and person that hurt you. For some of you I know this may be painful but remember you can't overcome what you don't face.

ANGELO M. SWINSON

I am praying for you right now that God will give you the boldness and strength even right now to complete this exercise and that it will be the beginning of your healing process and journey to recovery, in Jesus name I pray Amen.

Everything and every person that comes to your mind begin to write their name and the offense; doesn't matter if you need more paper get it all out. You can repeat this exercise as many times as needed in the event that everything doesn't comes back at once.

After writing all the names and the offense begin to call out their names and say I forgive them, keep in mind this is not for them but this is for you. Ex. 1: I forgive Jim for raping me as a child. Ex. 2: I forgive Jessica for cheating on me with my best friend Jackson. Ex. 3: I forgive my mother/father for never being a real parent in my life. Ex. 4: I forgive myself for believing I deserved all of this or that it was my fault.

NO MORE DYSFUNCTIONAL LOVE

If the person is still alive and the Lord leads you; you may even want to go to them or write them a letter just to say "I forgive you" if the person is deceased then saying it out loud from your spirit will suffice, only do this when you are ready and God has released you to do so. You can repeat this exercise as many times as needed until you feel you have totally been released from the pain of this hurt. Release all of the anger, bitterness, resentment and unforgiveness then after you have release it them then release yourself. The biggest trick of the enemy when it comes to forgiveness is letting it go, you have often heard the statement "I will forgive but I won't forget", you are not suppose to remember it to keep you your guards up but know that your experiences in life whether good or bad have taught you a valuable lesson and the scar is there as a reminder of where the Lord has brought you from and what you made it through. Don't allow your past to rob you of your future. It may look the same but yet be totally different; don't get distracted by the familiarity of the one experience with the new one. The enemy always tries to duplicate what God wants to do in your life so just because it may look the same makes sure you discern the situation before you automatically assume it's not God. You will know the difference. Rely on the Father, He won't lead you wrong, He is there with you every step of the way.

Holding on to my Deliverance

Prayer is the key. When you have been delivered from the hurt of your past, you will know it. The moment you see the person that hurt you or hear their name you will experience a peace like none other, you will no longer desire to run them over with your car or lash out at them but you will only want to pray for them, that place of hurt no longer controls you. You can breathe and the anxiety is gone and you whisper, "Thank you Jesus", welcome to total deliverance and freedom. Remember as in anything else the enemy will try to return to check your testimony to see if you are truly free and when he does you can boldly shout that pain doesn't live here anymore. But even if he comes back and there is residue remaining, there is still hope. Pray and release it every time it shows its face because whatever you feed that's what will grow. You can let go of what you want release, get it out of your spirit the minute God reveals to you that it is still there.

You may say this is easier said than done, and in your mind that may very well be true, but if you truly want to come out of this cycle you will fight for your God -ordained right to be free. Also it may be a good idea to journal. If you can't talk about it write about it, this is a good way to clear things out of your spirit as well it's like your road map to recovery. After writing it all out you can go back in the months or years and see your progression from where you were to where you have come to. Even if the progression is slow, that's fine taking your time, but be consistent. Understand that the Father paid the ultimate price so that you could be free, it's your blood bought right, so exercise the power and authority that was made available over two-thousand years ago....be free!

I pray even know that the Lord God will help you and strengthen you as you start your journey to healing. I pray that you will be totally honest with yourself and God as your pour out of your spirit the past hurts and pain, and if you happen to be the one that caused others hurt or pain that today you will forgive yourself and walk in the newness of live knowing that the Father has forgiven you and you no longer have to walk under the shadow of condemnation. I pray even know that every shackle of unforgiveness will lose their holds on you now, in the mighty name of Jesus. And I decree that you will love again and allow yourself to be loved, I pray that your trust is returning and the passion and desire to live is springing up in you even now. I pray that you will be loosed from the obligation of carrying this pain from this day forward even as you read this pray you are being set free even now, I speak into your spirit that Jesus Christ dies on the cross and took your pain that you could be free and I decree and declare in Jesus name that you are free indeed!!

CHAPTER THREE

NOT GIVING INTO TEMPTATION

"Good habits result from resisting temptation". - **Author Unknown**

What is temptation? It is defined as a desire to do something, especially something wrong or unwise. This chapter is very important in regards to maintaining a healthy union by not allow temptation to have a foothold. Temptation can come in many different forms. It is a tool that the enemy uses to test those who are in healthy relationships. The enemy never will tempt you with something that is not normally appealing to your menu.

I myself have been tempted, and not because I was looking for the temptation. The way I am able to overcome temptations that comes my way was first my relationship with God. I valued who God was in my life before anything. By doing this it would allow me to be faithful in my marriage due to my relationship with God. The second reason is because I am married to the love of my life. Deep down, I know there is nothing in this world that I would trade for the love of my life.

I take into consideration the position that I hold in the church. Not only am I a prophet of God, but I am also a shepherd over a flock. I then begin to look a little bit deeper into the importance of not falling victim to temptation, specifically the lure of deceptive and inappropriate relationships. Many of us are familiar with the story of King David and Bathsheba, and the sin he committed with her. However, what we don't hear about is the fact that because of David's sin, those that were connected to him had to pay a price.

We have to realize that temptation sometimes comes to see what you are made of. Sometimes the enemy uses things to test us to see if

NO MORE DYSFUNCTIONAL LOVE

we really love our spouses. Sometimes, temptation may come when things are going right; sometimes it may come when things are going bad. It is very important to know how to be strong during your time of testing.

Whenever you value these things over the temptation, you are able to defeat the temptation. It is very important to understand the difference between being tempted willing and unwillingly. Willing means you are hoping to be tempted so you can explore other options; however, being tempted unwillingly is being tempted by someone that you are not interested in. Temptation is not a problem – until you *yield*, or to given into, that temptation.

Let's look into a few of the reasons why some of us yield to temptation. Some of us yield to the temptation because there is something that we are lacking from their spouse. Some of the things that we could be lacking are communication, prayer, love, affection, support, or maybe even security. *Communication*, or the imparting or exchanging of information or news, is one of the most important things in any relationship. You will notice that communication is one of the topics that I will discuss a lot throughout this book.

Whenever there is a lack of communication, the enemy is given room to come in when that wedge has formed in the relationship. A couple that communicates a lot, knows their spouse better. They will be able to detect when something is wrong or a shifting has occurred. The only way to truly get to know your spouse is by communication. In order for the relationship to stand, communication has to be on the top of the list.

The next important thing is prayer. Whenever a couple doesn't pray together, they are then removing God from the equation. Prayer is a solemn request for help, or expression of thanks addressed to God or an object of worship. Matthew 26:41 says, "Watch and pray so that you will not fall into temptation. The spirit is willing, but the body is weak." The best way to keep a marriage or relationship strong is the unity through prayer. Whenever a couple prays together, they are allowing themselves to be open with God, and each other, about their issues.

Not only are they being open with God, but they are communicating with God concerning their relationship and putting Him in control of it. Additionally, another thing that is key in a successful marriage is the love. Love is an intense feeling of deep affection, and if one of the persons no longer feels the love of their spouse, they then feel neglected and rejected. Whenever a person feels rejected, they look for someone or something to make them feel accepted.

No one wants to feel lonely in any relationship. That is why it is very important for a couple to spend time together. This brings me to another important point: affection. Whenever a person lacks affection, they are going to search for it elsewhere. This is vital in a marriage. *Affection*, a gentle feeling of fondness or liking, doesn't always have to be intimacy; it can be shown in many different ways.

First and foremost, we have to realize that men and women have different ways that they show affection. For example, women may want to communicate and want the man to do things for her. A woman would rather be shown that you love her more than being told. In contrast, a man would like for the woman to allow him to feel the love that he has for her. If couples learn these steps early on, it will prevent many problems later.

Another key point to help avoid temptation is support. The word *support* is defined as bearing all or part of the weight of; to hold up. Whenever your spouse doesn't feel the support, they tend to feel unappreciated. This will cause that individual to long for the acceptance that they are not getting at home. Moreover, both parties would want to feel that they have security with you; *security,* being the state of freedom from danger or threat.

NO MORE DYSFUNCTIONAL LOVE

Whenever a person yields to temptation, it will undoubtedly give birth to something else down the road. The reason why it is important to avoid temptation is because it will start as one thing but become a completely different thing in the future. It is very important to weigh out the consequence, rather than the pleasure. Consequence and pleasure cannot be compared; they domino-effect each other.

It is very important to not allow yourself to become open to temptation in your life. The best way to avoid temptation is by maintaining intimacy and keeping the love fresh between you and your mate. Some of us have to allow ourselves to fall in love with our mate all over again. There are many creative ways to "keeping it fresh," and I will be discussing some of those methods. You must be innovative in how you choose to enhance your marriage!

One, rather important thing that you can do is spend more time together. By spending time together, it allows you as a couple to stay connected in a way that make temptation much less of an issue. It is important to go on trips, have a date night, read books together, and basically anything that will give you and your spouse time alone together. This allows you as a couple to grow together and spend quality time.

What I have learned is that whenever you are so in love with the person God has ordained for your life, temptation is sure to make an attempt to rear its head. It is very important that we are not persuaded by the temptation. However, once again, if we were in a place of true happiness, then the temptation would not be an issue. It is only when the happiness is lacking, or when someone is not totally satisfied and complete with the mate the God has for them, that temptation becomes a problem.

The bible tells us that we already have the victory, even when we are tempted.

NO MORE DYSFUNCTIONAL LOVE
1 Corinthians 10:13

"No temptation has seized you except what is common to man. And God is faithful; he will not let you be tempted beyond what you can bear. But when you are tempted, he will also provide a way out so that you can stand up under it."

By applying the word of God over our lives, we protect ourselves from the snares the enemy may have set before us. For some of us, the reason why we are defeated when temptation comes is because we don't shut the door of the temptation. The longer you dwell on it, the more alive the temptation becomes.

Reflecting on what a friend of mines told me, to keep in mind that my thoughts and choices affect my actions. If you allow it to be in your thoughts, it will affect the choices you make, which then become the actions you have taken. These are some of the most powerful nuggets that can be offered to couples that want to have a prosperous marriage. It's not always the issue we should focus on, but rather the solution to help resolve these issues. I believe that the more help that is offered to couples, the better they will become.

If they are taught the value of marriage and covenant, they will not fall victim to temptation so easily. They will look at the overall picture, versus a few minutes of pleasure. They will look at how this could affect them and their mate in the long run. I believe that giving into temptation is a selfish act; it is very important to know that it doesn't just affect you. It could damage everything that you have worked so hard for.

We must realize God honors faithfulness when we are tested. The scripture tells us in

James 1:12

"Blessed is the man who perseveres under trial, because when he has stood the test, he will receive the crown of life that God has promised to those who love him."

When we value our relationship with our spouse as a promise, we then handle the promise better. Often times used yet not always fully comprehended, a promise is defined as a declaration or assurance that one will do a particular thing or that guarantees that a particular thing will happen.

A real marriage requires two people that want to make it work. If we allow ourselves to possess a selfless mindset and truly consider the blessing that comes with being married, we can overcome any obstacle. It is extremely important to know what the scriptures tell us in

Mark 10:9

"What therefore God hath joined together, let not man put asunder." With the help of God, there is nothing in the world that we can't overcome. "

Are you a person that is dealing with temptation right now? Are you looking for a way to escape? Is there a door or a window that you have allowed to form that is causing you to feel weak?

ANGELO M. SWINSON

Are you feeling vulnerable and afraid that you may fall victim to what the enemy is sending you way? Pray this prayer that will help you strengthen you spirit-man and cause your flesh to die down:

Father God, in the name of Jesus, I come to you humbly and broken as I know how. I come to you in desperation of your touch and your deliverance. I ask that you give me power over my thoughts and dominion over my flesh. God I ask that you renew my mind and make me a new creature. God I ask that you take this urge away from me.

Deliver me from anything that is familiar. God remove this desire that will separate me from you. Fill me with your love and your spirit. God I ask that you saturate this room with your presence. Bring me to a place and maturity and boldness, so that when I am under attack, I am reminded of your word.

Plant your word inside my heart that I won't sin against you .God I bless you in advance for total deliverance and restoration from every area of weakness. I pray that you allow me to walk in holy

NO MORE DYSFUNCTIONAL LOVE

boldness and overcome everything that is sent my way. God I ask that you bring me to a place of total brokenness in you, in Jesus name I pray. Psalm 51:10 "Create in me a clean heart, O God; and renew a right spirit within me." Amen.

CHAPTER FOUR

AFTER THE TURBULENCE

"We must develop and maintain the capacity to forgive. He who is devoid of the power to forgive is devoid of the power to love. There is some good in the worst of us and some evil in the best of us."
- Martin Luther King, Jr.

When you think of turbulence what is it that first comes to mind? Some of us may think of flying in an airplane. Others may look at it as an imbalance in the movement of the plane. Yet, some may look at it as something that causes us to be fearful while flying. I have a different outlook when it comes to turbulence and the ultimate purpose of it.

This is a chapter of redemption after the shaking. We will go in depth about how a covenant can face ups and downs, and still survive. The word

NO MORE DYSFUNCTIONAL LOVE

shaking means to cause to tremble or vibrate. A relationship or marriage that goes through a testing time is considered a relationship in turbulence. We look at it as *turbulence*, which is anything that changes the mood of the relationship, because that is precisely what is occurring.

Turbulence, in my opinion, is something that comes to change the dynamics of a relationship. It is something that comes to bring out new dimensions in your relationship. For example, you never know a person until they are under pressure. Some of us crack under pressure and can't handle the weight of life.

I believe that there is some turbulence that should be expected, and comes with the territory. We should look at turbulence as an indication that your relationship is headed higher or getting closer to your place of purpose. Whenever a boxer has to prepare for a fight, he trains with victory in mind. It is very important to lay a foundation that can withhold the rockiness when turbulence comes. Whenever your foundation is laid in God, there will be nothing that can shake it, no matter how strong the storm is. A *foundation* is the lowest, load-bearing part of a building, typically below ground level; words of wisdom, with that in mind, would be to build, build, and build more. Whenever you continue to build something, it won't be easily broken. Whenever you are faced with unfortunate circumstances, the strength you have stored will kick in. The only way to overcome tests and trials is to properly prepare.

We do understand that some days will seem to be sweet and sour. Preparation is the key overcoming turbulence that comes in your relationship. The purpose of this is to maintain balance and prepare you for what lies ahead. It allows couples to get to know each other on another level, deeper than what is learned on a regular basis. You can never win a battle unless you know you have someone that is willing to fight with you.

NO MORE DYSFUNCTIONAL LOVE

The purpose of turbulence is for couples to get to know their spouses beyond the surface of their relationship. This is a time in which the two of you should strengthen one another. The only time a couple gets defeated during turbulence is when they draw back from one another. The scriptures tell us in

Deuteronomy 32:30

"How could one person chase a thousand of them, and two people put ten thousand to flight, unless their Rock had sold them, unless the LORD had given them up?"

Whenever the two of you come together, there is nothing that can stop, hinder, block, or prevent your marriage from succeeding.

Case in point: things can be going perfectly fine then out of nowhere almost everything seems to take a shift. You can be in love today and then tomorrow, it seems as though the love isn't there. It's not that the love has left the relationship, but rather it is that the love is being *challenged*, or lacking or deficient in a specified respect. Likened to school, whenever you were in class and took a test, you were tested based on the knowledge you already learned.

Your love is tested simply to see if it is really present. *Turbulence*, or a state or condition of confusion, movement, or agitation; disorder, is never intended to destroy but rather enhance the couple. Other types of turbulence include changing wind-speeds, combined with an unstable air layer, causes "waves" of up and down motion within this air layer. Spiritual insight tells us that these changes happen in order to get you to where you are going as a couple.

For a moment, consider turbulence as part of the process. *Process* is defined as performing a series of mechanical or chemical operations in order to change or preserve it. The scriptures tell us in

James 1:12

"Blessed is a man who perseveres under trial; for once he has been approved, he will receive the crown

NO MORE DYSFUNCTIONAL LOVE

of life, which [the Lord] has promised to those who love Him."

Perseverance, or steadfastness in doing something despite difficulty or delay in achieving success, is the key to surviving your season of turbulence.

Now allow me to introduce you to a couple by the name of Willie and Angela. Willie and Angela met while working at a store together in 1994. They started dating shortly after they met each other. They dated for about 8 years, off and on. In October 2002, they decided to get married and take their relationship to another level. They have now been married for over ten years now.

Willie and Angela began to face some turbulence in their marriage, which caused much shaking to take place. Problems began to arise when they allowed work or ministry to interfere with their personal lives. Willie recalled that things began to become shaky when the ministry they were attending started to shift. Angela started to get mistreated while attending this ministry, which caused a *strain* (force to make a strenuous or unusually great effort) in their marriage.

Things began to get worse as time progressed. Angela decided to leave the ministry, but Willie stayed. This caused a wedge to grow between the both of them. There was a pastor-friend that Angela would go to for advice. She would go off to the pastor's house, where other members who had issues with that ministry, were going as well.

They would all sit around and talk about the problems they had. Because these issues were only communicated at this pastor's house, the wedge between Willie and Angela steadily expanded. At the time, Angela really couldn't say anything to Willie because he was the pastor's right-hand man. As a result, they became a divided household. Angela's pastor-friend would tell her that Willie chose the ministry over his wife. This caused Angela to feel like Willie didn't support her. Other issues and turbulence ensued between the two of them.

Like a domino effect, trust issues began to arise. I would like to call this time period the "Trust Factor," in which trust is not where it should be amongst husband and wife. Willie wouldn't know where Angela was at times, and Angela would start suspecting Willie of being unfaithful and having affairs on her. This critical time in their marriage caused the both of them to nearly get a divorce.

The way they communicated with each other had completely changed. I am a firm believer if your home is not in order, then nothing else will be. They both decided to stick to the commitment of the vows they made on their wedding day. Willie decided to stay because he felt like it wasn't the will of God for him to leave, but at the time also felt like it was meant for him to stay by his pastor's side instead of leaving the ministry along with his wife.

When his wife decided to leave the church, it should have been a joint decision. I am firm believer that if someone were affecting my spouse, then I would need to try to work it out with my spouse. Whenever we say, "I do" we are now bonded with this person and are now supposed to protect the person we are with. The scriptures tell us in

Matthew 6:21

"For where your treasure is, there will your heart be also."

If you truly love someone you will fight and defend them. Anything that is not worth fighting for is not worth having. If you don't stand for something, you will eventually fall for anything. We have to look at it this way: at the end of the day, it is you and your spouse. First, we must make sure that we are pleasing God, and then we must make sure that we are in right standing with our spouses. Everyone and everything else comes after that.

NO MORE DYSFUNCTIONAL LOVE

I do understand that many of us have been taught the other way for years. However, I would like to re-program your mind to do it God's way. For many years, I would say, we have been going *against the grain*, or to go contrary to someone's natural disposition. This is the foundation that Willie and Angela's marriage original had. *I take thee to be my wedded spouse, to have and to hold from this day <u>forward</u>, for better for worse, for richer, for poorer, in sickness and in health, to love and to cherish, till death us do part, according to God's holy ordinance, and thereto I pledge you my love and faithfulness.* By reciting these words, you *vow*, or make a solemn promise, to protect and to love that person you are married to.

Things began to eventually get better in their marriage when they had a discussion about the ministry and what had taken place. Willie took the time to listen to Angela express what had affected her. By him simply listening, the healing process was able to begin. They began to talk about the situation and what they felt, collectively, wasn't right. Willie felt like they really needed to focus on hearing from God for instructions, so he began to get deeper into his word and increased his prayer time.

The Lord spoke to him and told him it was time to leave that ministry. The both of them were finally able to come to a mutual understanding concerning the ministry they were attending. This was something that opened Willie's eyes to the bigger picture. It allowed him to look at what was more important: his marriage or the ministry that he was in. I believe this is a critical question that a lot of us should ask ourselves: "Is it worth me losing everything?"

Time needed to be taken to allow Angela to be healed from the emotional wounds that were there as a result. They apologized to each other and decided to put that behind them. They are now expecting a new bundle of joy, and their relationship, love, and marriage are in a much better state now. As I stated earlier, turbulence can also come and shift things for the better.

Now that they have encountered the rough side of marriage, they officially understand what it takes to overcome it. Now that they have let go of what has happened, the blessings of God have overflowed in their marriage. The scriptures tell us in

Philippians 2:2
"Then make my joy <u>complete</u> by being like-minded, having the same love, being one in spirit and of one mind."

Whenever you put these things into place, you can then enjoy the blessings that God has for you in your marriage. Willie and Angela have ultimately learned how to keep the faith when turbulent situations arise.

Each couple has to be willing to grow and move on after the turbulence has taken place. They have to be able to figure out strategic ways to overcome the pain and disappointment. They have to remember what it takes to overcome the rough times that they were faced with, and realize that what they went through is to help someone else who may be experiencing the same thing. The presence of turbulence can show you how to preserve those things that are important.

Turbulence is not something that is permanent, but rather temporary for a specific purpose. Remember, there is a difference between permanent and temporary. Permanent is forever; temporary is seasonal, and the intent of it is to build you, not break you. Turbulence comes to make your marriage better, stronger, and healthier by what you overcome. Always remember that turbulence doesn't come to make your marriage fail.

CHAPTER FIVE

WAITING ON THE ONE

*"In all the world, there is no heart for me like yours. In all the world, there is no love for you like mine". **-Maya Angelou***

This is probably one of my favorite chapters of the book. This particular topic is very personal to me because of what I experienced while waiting on the "One." Some of us have the fairytale story of how they married their high school sweetheart, and how they lived happily ever after. Unfortunately, that is not how I found the "One" God had for me. Can you remember being in a place waiting for the mate that God had for you? I would like to share some deep insight into my personal experiences, as well as the experiences of others that I know.

This chapter will help you overcome some challenges, and answer questions concerning selecting the right mate – the very reason why this book was created. It was written to bring clarity to those needing confirmation, which means confirming something or the state of being confirmed – giving a person the assurance that they are making the right decision. Suffice it to say, this chapter that will cause you to look at the word "confirmation" differently from this day forward.

Now, I must express (and stress) that there is a difference between "confirmation" and "validation." Validation is the act of validating; finding or testing the truth of something. Personally, I believe the best ministry that a person can move or operate in is transparency; it is the only way others can become free. I can remember personally, and even in conversations with others, how wanting and needing validation from people ruined the moment with the mate God had me.

NO MORE DYSFUNCTIONAL LOVE

I agree with those I spoke with, that the reason why it ruined their moment is because they allowed the opinions of others to persuade them into going with *those* opinions, rather than *God's* opinion. It is very important to understand the difference between the "One" and a "good person." I would like to pause for a moment and break down the difference between a good person and the "One" that God has for you. For example, a person maybe a "good person", but the question is, are they good for you? In the past, I myself have been involved with good people; but they were perfect for someone else.

Good means to be desired or approved of; *perfect* means all the required or desirable elements, qualities, or characteristics – as good as it is possible to be. It is very important to understand why it is not good to look for VALIDation, but rather, for CONFIRMation. Validation is the vehicle used to solidify the fact that you are looking for someone to approve who God has for you. Confirmation, on the other hand, is good if you get it but you will not base your relationship on it. The reason it is very important not to look for validation and confirmation is because everyone may not have your best interest at heart.

On a personal note, I can remember when I first connected with the "One." I received word that there were some that was coming to try to persuade me that she was not it.

I met a couple from Florida named Phillip and Sandra. They met at a church that they were attending while they were living in Florida. Sandra's best friend at the time had major surgery and came over to Phillip's parent's house to recuperate after the surgery. Sandra was over every day to help her friend with the healing process. Phillip and Sandra had no idea about their future union. They were attending the same church for almost five years and had never noticed each other.

As time passed, they became very close friends. They eventually realized that they liked each other, but had kept it hidden from one another. When the two of them finally started dating, they had no idea the amount of warfare they would face from the ministry they were members of. This particular church picked someone else for Sandra to marry, and even selected a different woman for Phillip to marry. They did everything they could to break Phillip and Sandra up. The intercessory council was even praying that their relationship would fail, on the instructions they received from the Bishop of the church.

As Phillip began preparing to propose to Sandra, their pastor made them break up. During the three weeks of separation, Phillip pursued Sandra again and said, "I want you in my life. When are we going to get back together?" After three more months of dating, Phillip proposed to Sandra and a year later, they were married. Confirmation was obviously not the issue for them. Phillip knew that the person placed in front of him was a union ordained by God. The Lord had made all of the signs clear for them concerning their relationship.

The warfare they faced while being together indicated that it was God-ordained. Sandra loved the way Phillip chased her, so of course she was waiting for him to make the move again to see if he really loved her. The fire intensified after they got married, and it wasn't until then that they began to question whether they heard from God. Later they both left the ministry they were a part of, upon meeting their current pastor. The very first prophetic word they received from the new pastor was that God said not to question this marriage ever again, and that HE put them together for HIS purpose!

It is very important to stand on the promises of God. I also believe that what is not worth fighting for is really not worth having; if a person doesn't stand for anything they will eventually fall for anything. It is also important to know the treasure that you have in your mate, and it is your job to protect the blessing that God has given you. In order to maintain a solid stance, it is important to have standards. Whenever standards are in effect,

NO MORE DYSFUNCTIONAL LOVE

you won't settle for an ordinary, coach ticket when you could have a first-class, luxury seat.

Now of course, I am not saying that you should be materialistic. I will state that it is important to have some standards while waiting. What I have learned is that many of us have not prayed and consulted God on the direction we should go. When someone connects with the "One," the "One" should have the natural ability to take them from one place in their life to the next. Even when you may be empty, this person is able to make you feel the fullness of life through the love of Christ. In order to really be able to love someone else, you must be filled with the love of Christ.

Until you are able to identify your true identity through Christ, it is impossible to effectively love someone else unconditionally. That person should make you glow and feel special, In essence, the person that He has for you should cause you to want to do more and become all that God has for you.

The "One" may not necessarily be perfect; in fact, that person won't be perfect. Yet, he or she will be perfect for you! They should be able to wake up things you didn't know could resurrect, and will be able to make you smile when no one else can.

The bible tells us in

Mark 10:9

"What therefore God hath joined together, let not man put asunder."

Being asunder is to be apart, divided. So, in other words don't let anyone separate you from what God has for you. If you allow others to cause you to move out of timing, it can make you miss out on what God has for you. For example, if someone tells you that your mate is not not for you, based off of flesh and not godly wisdom consider it being a hidden agenda or motive. When this occurs, it can cause you to not have happiness, while that person is able to move on with their lives, and possibly find their ordained mate that God has for them. I can remember while waiting for my mate, God prepared me emotionally so that I could be able to effectively minister to her.

I'm reminded of when I first met my wife. We were friends at the time; I had recently come out of a relationship, and she as well. However, because we both had already prayed to God for what we wanted, it didn't take long for us to recognize that our blossoming friendship was God-ordained. We began to truly value and protect what God had put together. This further brings me to my next topical point: validation from others.

Some may not have your best interests at heart when it comes to validation. I can remember when I was looking for the "One" who is now my lovely wife. There were some seasons that I had to go through to get me to that point. These seasons helped me prepare myself mentally, physically, and spiritually for her arrival and presence in my life. Now of course, I was not the only one who went through some seasons; she also had her share of experiences and seasons before I came along. The seasons that I am speaking of are the times and struggles that push us in the face of God.

Seasons are the four divisions of the year marked by particular weather patterns and daylight hours. It is very important for a person to know what season that they are in. We do understand that everyone is in a different season of his or her life. Some of us are in the season of being broken – having been fractured or damaged, and no longer in one piece or in working order; others, moving into a season of restoration, which is undoubtedly the obverse of brokenness, being the return of something to a former owner, place, or condition.

Some of us are in the preparation season, which is the process of making ready, or being made ready, for use. The rest of us, if not in the previous, are in our due season, which is the position to be expected at or planned for at a certain time. This is the season in which you have been thoroughly processed, and now you are ready for the "One" in your life. All of these seasons are designed to come to mature and prepare us for the "One." Now, back to testifying about when I was waiting for her!

I realized the importance of knowing what you want in life, and fully understanding what you pray to God for. After consistent prayer, I made it a point to stand firm in my faith on what I consulted the Lord about. My prayer was to be able to know what to look for based on what I had asked for; it is important to understand what and who the "One" is.

Many of us look for something that is already packaged perfectly, and tied with a ribbon. The "One" may not come the way you expect her or him to come. The "One" could be someone you would have never expected.

Waiting on "the person God has ordained for you" has become one of the most popular phrases in the body of Christ. Some of us are looking for someone to be exactly like us with no flaws.

The "One" may be someone that is the opposite of what you are used to. Think about it: would there be any balance if you married someone exactly like you?

Balance comes into play to bring an even distribution of weight, enabling someone or something to remain upright and steady. Don't you think that life would be pretty boring if you insisted on dating someone who is exactly like you?

Yes, it is possible to have the "One" that is ordained to be with you! There shall be some experiences before the right mate comes; everyone will have endured a process in which they are positioned and put in place to receive the person God has created for them. We must understand that the scripture tells us in

Proverbs 18:22

"Whosoever finds a wife finds a good thing, and obtains favor of the LORD."

NO MORE DYSFUNCTIONAL LOVE

I believe that in order to have that "One" that is God sent you, you must first position yourself for the "One." God will not send the "One" until you are ready for them. We covered a lot in the previous chapters such as communication, past hurt, affection; and credit.

In order to be able to have the "One," your maturity has to be in place to even possess the ability to walk with the "One." The "One" represents the love of God and you will be able to enjoy them without any hindrances because emotional healing would have already taken place.

Additionally, whenever the "One" comes, we have to make sure that we protect what God has given us. For example, everyone may not want to celebrate that person being in your life, but you have to know without a shadow of a doubt that they are it, and that you will not be persuaded otherwise. When the "One" comes your world will begin to change, but nothing should be able to alter your thoughts about that person.

It is also important to love yourself while waiting on the "One." This is will prepare you to love that person the right way. Prepare is to make (something) ready for use or consideration. Preparing yourself for your mate allows the process for your mate to select you. Keep in mind the importance of being healed from emotional wounds; the "One" should not to have to pay for someone else mistakes.

As I conclude this chapter, there are just a few things I want you remember while waiting for the person God has ordained for you. Remember that it is your job to allow yourself to become the one that can be selected to be the "One." This means to prepare yourself spiritually, physically, and emotionally so that after you are processed, you are able to recognize the "One" because you are also that person's "One."

CHAPTER SIX

INSPITE OF UNCONDITIONAL LOVE

"Love is the condition in which the happiness of another person is essential to your own".
-Robert Heinlein

The phrase, "In-spite-of love," can be translated to, "No matter how imperfect the person is, you love them unconditionally; no matter how much they may be lacking, you love them just the same; no matter where they may be immature, you love them beyond their mindset." Even if they don't treat you well, you love – in spite of. In essence, this phrase proposes that even though they are not perfect, you love them just the way they are.

Unconditional love is not simply limited to mistakes and errors; you can love someone when they may not have. For example, that person maybe unemployed, but that doesn't stop your love. Unconditional (or in-spite-of) love shows them that you will love them through the process of finding a job. In-spite-of love shows a person that even if they were to get ill, your love for them would never change. In-spite-of love doesn't have limitations or boundaries.

Let me introduce to you a couple by the name of Janice and James. Janice grew up in the great city of Miami, Florida. She decided that she wanted a change in her life, so she relocated to Chicago, Illinois, when she was just 18 years-old. She later gave her life to the Lord and then became heavily involved in the church. She already had to two children out of wedlock when she met a man by the name of James. Janice and James dated for awhile before they got married. At first, Janice didn't want to marry James because she didn't feel that he was right for her. Janice and James had been living together for quite some time now. As Janice began to seek the face of God more she desired to be filled with the spirit of God. Upon getting filled with the spirit of God she then realized that she could no longer live with James and not be married to him. Janice felt that God spoke to her and told her that James wasn't her husband – however, James told her otherwise.

Janice's pastor told her that she was just a babe in Christ and that God didn't tell her that James wasn't her husband. Janice wanted to please God and be in accordance with the spiritual counseling she received from her pastor, so she decided to marry James. During this time, James wasn't saved or in the church like Janice was. James never hindered her from doing anything that God called her to do, but he also chose to remain in the background as God continued to elevate Janice in ministry.

As God began to stir up the gift on the inside of Janice, it gave her a great zeal concerning the things of God. The challenges came as she began to seek God, and as she began to be used in the ministry. James didn't have the same zeal and passion concerning the things of God. This caused James to become *distant*, or far away in space or time, from Janice.

James didn't mind Janice being who she was in God. He allowed himself to occupy time finding other things to do, while she was doing the work of Lord. James began to do things that didn't include his family, nor did they include God. Even though James had a lack of interest in church, Janice still didn't leave him. This is the perfect example of what unconditional love is.

Not even years into their marriage did James begin to go back to partying, having affairs, and even smoking marijuana. This is what created the open door to a lot of confusion in their home. The more Janice would stand in the gap, the more things seemed like they were getting worse. Whenever Janice would seek the face of God, He would reply by stating that this was the result of her disobedience. He would also remind Janice of a familiar verse of scripture that says, *"and he said unto me, my grace is sufficient for thee: for my strength is made perfect in weakness."* Most gladly therefore will I rather glory in my infirmities, that the power of Christ may rest upon me."

After two years of marriage, the relentless affairs continued, with Janice contracting a venereal disease. At this point, Janice had to make a decision as a parent, wife, mother, and a pastor. Did she want to remain in the marriage? This would be the most life-changing decision she would have to make, and it would surely affect her as a person.

She felt that the reason she was going through this situation was to overcome it for someone else. She weighed what she was going through, to be deeper than her role as a pastor or parent. Those things were very important to her, and assisted in her decision to stay married to James – even though it would cost her more money and cause even more pain. She felt as though she would be a failure if she left James. At this point she was released by God to leave James, but she decided to stay with him instead. What would those that are connected to her say if she went through with the divorce?

Notice that Janice has shown great faithfulness towards James, even though James had broken the covenant with his affairs and *infidelity*, which is the action or state of being unfaithful to a spouse or other sexual partner. Janice encouraged herself to stand for her marriage even though James wasn't meeting her half-way.

Even when Janice decided to stay, things still didn't change; James continued with his infidelity. What helped Janice through this process was the word of God. She allowed herself to be buried in the presence of God during her time of testing. The bible and church became her comfort and her sense of peace.

While she sought the face of God even the more, God would then reveal the plan of the enemy in others' lives. The scripture tells us in John 10:10, "The thief cometh not, but for to steal, and to kill, and to destroy: I am come that they might have life, and that they might have it more abundantly." She wanted to use what the enemy was doing in her marriage as a reason to minister the word of God even the more. By doing this, her will to stay in her marriage increased, and displayed strength to others.

As time progressed, James' behavior became worse and worse. James had become bolder in his relationships with other women, even when Janice would try to communicate with him, asking him why he insisted on acting the way he was. James would always reply by stating that he didn't know why he did what he did. It got so bad until the women that James was involved with would eventually start calling their house.

James' affairs got so bad that he was unable to help pay the bills at their home. The result of James' actions caused them to lose their new home to foreclosure. This took place because James would spend his money on other women rather than taking care of his home. This caused Janice to go into a place of depression and disappointment, causing her to become very bitter.

After being faced with all that she went through, Janice then began to go back to God about her situation. She told Him that she was tired of going through with James. God would respond back to her, like always, and tell her that because she disobeyed Him and married James, this is the price that she will have to pay as a result. God would also remind her that His grace is sufficient, and that His strength is made perfect in her weakness.

NO MORE DYSFUNCTIONAL LOVE
2 Corinthians 12:9

"Most gladly therefore will I rather boast in my weaknesses, that the power of Christ may rest upon me."

During the time that Janice was going through, no one close to her knew what she was facing. Everyone was able to see that she was anointed, but no one could see the pain on the inside of her. Even those that were very close to her weren't able to detect that she was "leading while bleeding." Not even her children or family knew what Janice was going through. She would travel all over the world and minister the word of God, and her ministry would bless people tremendously. While demonstrating the power of God, no one could tell she was crying out for help in the midst of it.

Often times, Janice would go back to the pastor that married them and tell him what she was going through with James. The pastor would always tell her that it was of God and that she needed to stay with her husband. He never told her that she might have made a mistake, or that it wasn't God's will. Janice then decided that she needed to continue to stay with James. She decided that she would love James in spite of, because she didn't want to let those down that looked up to her.

Janice decided to suffer in spite of the pain she was faced with. No matter how bad it got, she often asked herself what the church would think. *What would my children think of me if I got a divorce? What about the souls that are connected to my ministry.* Janice considered these things while solidifying her decision to stay with James.

As a result of the way her life was going, Janice became even angrier with James. Then more trouble came. James got shot while trying to break up a fight. He was hospitalized for an entire year after the shooting. After being in a coma for 3 months, James stated that he kept seeing fire all around him during that time.

NO MORE DYSFUNCTIONAL LOVE

James was released from the hospital, but was unable to take care of himself. James could no longer come and go as he pleased; he had to depend on Janice to help him. He has not been the same since his shooting, and is not able to live the life he once enjoyed.

This story has taught me the value of forgiving others unconditionally. The word unconditional is defined as not being subjected to any conditions. Essentially, you love the person no matter how imperfect they maybe. The scripture tells us in

1 Corinthians 7:14

"The unbelieving husband is sanctified by the wife, and the unbelieving wife is sanctified by the husband: else were your children unclean; but now are they holy."

CHAPTER SEVEN
THE ADVICE

"A successful marriage requires falling in love many times, always with the same person".
- Unknown

I believe that the best advice is the advice that comes from experience. I have always heard that you can never effectively witness something you have never lived. I would like to take the opportunity to share some of my insight, advice, and observations, with hopes that it will help you have a long and prosperous marriage. I believe that this will not only aid in showing you how to have a strong marriage, but also help those who are struggling to keep their marriage alive.

NO MORE DYSFUNCTIONAL LOVE

It is very important to get to know your spouse before marriage, beyond just knowing their name, favorite color, and age. Get to know them on a deeper level; discover what their likes and dislikes are. Find out what they love about you, and find out what their biggest pet-peeve is. If you take some of this advice in with an open mind, I guarantee that you will experience a new level of love and intimacy that God has destined for your marriage to embody.

The scriptures tell us in

Amos 3:3
"Can two walk together, except they are agreed?"

Find out if both of you are going the same direction in life. This will allow the two of you the ability to see if you can come together for a specific purpose.

Now let's shift for a second and talk about the difference between advice and opinion. When problems arise, we tend to go to people for advice, and it is usually their opinion that is offered. There are a few things that we need to consider during the process of seeking advice from others. We need to ask ourselves if this is godly advice, or if it is an opinion formed from personal feelings. We also have to ask ourselves if that person is genuinely trying to help, or if they have a hidden agenda. Additionally, we have to be very careful who we share our issues with because everyone doesn't have our best interest at heart. *Advice* is defined as guidance or recommendations concerning prudent, future action, whereas the word *opinion* is a view or judgment formed about something, not necessarily based on fact or knowledge. Know that when you receive advice, you are receiving guidance; however, when you receive an opinion you are receiving something that is not necessarily going to help you.

NO MORE DYSFUNCTIONAL LOVE

I believe that if any couple is considering marriage, they should look into counseling. Counseling is the provision of assistance and guidance in resolving personal, social, or psychological problems and difficulties. Through personal experience, I have discovered a lot of things that normally go unmentioned or not completely discussed, are the very focal points in counseling sessions, such as: religious background, money management, intimacy, children, goals, dreams, and so much more. This allows both couples to see what each other's points of view are and how they would handle certain life issues. Each couple will then be able to see if they are open to discuss any and everything, and therefore possess the ability of working together to maintain their marriage. This builds up a confidence and trust in that partner, which also builds on the friendship aspect of their union.

Proverbs 11:14

"Where no counsel is, the people fall: but in the multitude of counselors there is safety."

Counseling helps reinforce the basis of a prosperous marriage.

 Communication is a term that is used so much throughout this book. Being one the essential characteristics of any healthy relationship, I will constantly refer back to it. Again, communication is such a powerful tool for couples to utilize in their quest of getting to know one another. By communicating, you are able to build a confidence in your spouse and allow them to be able to trust you. Praying together is another important aspect in the maintenance of your relationship. It is not only a form of communication that both of you as husband and wife do together, but you also involve your Heavenly Father in your affairs, and He is truly the best counselor and mediator in your corner!

NO MORE DYSFUNCTIONAL LOVE

Now, allow me to introduce you to an awesome couple that I know: LaShaun and Andrew. They met on a popular Internet site, years ago. LaShaun lived in a different state than Andrew while they were dating. Their chance meeting occurred one day when Andrew needed someone to edit his paper. He decided to post a status regarding this on a social network site that he frequented. No one responded immediately, so Andrew reposted the same status again out of desperation because it needed to be properly edited before he turned it in to his professor. LaShaun noticed the post and decided to respond back, agreeing to edit it for him. By this time, LaShaun only had an hour to look over it, but was able to get it back to him ten minutes before it was due. Andrew received a passing grade but did not relay the message to LaShaun. After some time had passed, LaShaun inboxes Andrew to see how he was doing and if he received a passing grade on his paper. Andrew replied with a "yes", and commended her on a job well done. They continued corresponding with each other for a few months, and eventually realized there was an attraction almost a year later. Andrew constantly found himself going to her page to check up on her and admire her pictures, realizing how beautiful she was. One day, LaShaun inboxed Andrew asking him to pray for her because she was going through some things in her life, including getting out of a terrible marriage. Andrew offered his phone number to her. Later that night LaShaun gave Andrew a call and as soon as they greeted one another, it was like they had known each other for years.

As a side note, I must make mention of the fact that Andrew was not in a serious relationship at the time, but had "options" that he kept in touch with. When he and LaShaun began to talk on a regular basis, he realized that those "options" were no longer potential factors in his life. As time progressed, Lashaun and Andrew began to seriously date, long-distance. During that year of dating, the two of them only met on two occasions before actually getting married to one another, with Andrew deciding to propose via telephone on Resurrection Sunday. Lashaun immediately accepted. Andrew heard the Lord speak to him, telling him to leave everything behind and stay with a relative until they got married, nearly two months later. After their wedding, they immediately began doing ministry together. Since both had experience working in ministry before, it was easier for them to come together in a church leadership setting. Because they had prayed and fasted together, they knew they were able to face anything when they came together because of the foundation they laid before they got married.

After their first year of marriage, things began to shift to a greater level in their lives. During their second year, they began seeking the Lord concerning His will for their lives – whether He wanted them to stay in their current location, Georgia, or move to do ministry elsewhere. As they began to fast and pray on a 30-day consecration, the Lord spoke clear directions for them to remain in Georgia and start a ministry together.

When they decided to step out and trust the voice of God, things in their life and marriage would never be the same. Although they were comfortable with traveling and ministering locally, they understood and began moving in the true meaning of *accountability*, or the responsibility to someone or for some activity. They didn't second-guess their choice because they knew that they were on one accord between themselves and God when He put it on their heart and mind to start a church. They are now happily married with three children and a growing ministry.

Shifting gears a bit, I want to mention another key aspect within a healthy marriage: romance. After discussing the spiritual factors, let's focus on the affectionate side of marriage. When we first meet our mates, many of us do everything we can to *impress* that person, or make (someone) feel admiration and respect. Never lose this passion and make sure you always try to find new ways to increase the love you have for someone.

The scriptures tell us in

Ephesians 5:25-27

"Husbands, love your wives, even as Christ also loved the church, and gave himself for it; That he might sanctify and cleanse it with the washing of water by the word, That he might present it to himself a glorious church, not having spot, or wrinkle, or any such thing; but that it should be holy and without blemish."

Men, make your lady feel like she has security and shelter with you – like God has given you a queen, and you treasure her as such. It is our duty as their husbands to make them feel like they are the most special women on earth; not just by words, but also by our actions. Always keep in mind that "love" is a verb.

Ladies, it is your duty to make the man feel like he is the king of your castle. The scriptures tell us in the description of what virtuous women's characteristics are,

Proverbs 31:11-31

"The heart of her husband trusts in her, and he will have no lack of gain. She does him good, and not harm, all the days of her life. She seeks wool and flax, and works with willing hands. She is like the ships of the merchant; she brings her food from afar. She rises while it is yet night and provides food for her household and portions for her maidens."

Ladies, be the cultivators and helpmeets of your husband, pushing him to be all that he can be.

Find ways that you know will make feel like on one else can. Balance is important because this will give the enemy no room to be able to creep into what God has ordained. It is very important to never stop loving and showing affection for one another. Always find ways to continue to grow and learn together. Try to remember what made you fall in love in the first place. Make plans to together for the future and where you are headed together. The scriptures tell us in

Proverbs 29:18

"Where there is no vision, the people perish: but he that keepeth the law, happy is he."

Always remember that if you love each other, you can overcome anything. Remember to listen to each other and be considerate of one another's feelings. Never be afraid to ask for ways that you can improve in your marriage. Be an observer of your spouse; get to know them as a person emotionally, physically, and most of all, spiritually. Find out what makes them smile, what makes them cry, what makes them upset, and everything else in between.

Do everything in your power to build up your spouse every day. Remember there is power in unity and strength when you pray together. No matter what you are facing, continue to build each other up in times of testing. The scriptures tell us in

Proverbs 14:1

"Every wise woman buildeth her house: but the foolish plucketh it down with her hands."

No matter what it looks like, always speak the word of God over your marriage.

Proverbs 18:21

"Death and life are in the power of the tongue: and they that love it shall eat the fruit thereof."

Remember to be wise about those you choose to share your trials with during your marriage. This is one of the ways that you protect the spouse that God has given you.

When the storms of life come, make each other feel important. Encourage them that the two of you shall get through it together. Allow me to suggest some things that will help keep the fire lit in your marriage, regardless of good and bad times. It is very important that whenever you become

NO MORE DYSFUNCTIONAL LOVE

married, you never forget to continue dating your spouse; every couple should have a designated date night.

A date night is a night that is designed for the couple to spend some alone time together outside of the house, with no other duties or distractions to be concerned with. If you have children, it is even more so important to always have time for yourselves to come together. This is a time where the two of you can love on one another, and be able to discuss how things are going in your lives, individually and collectively. This is a good time to have each other's undivided attention. This gives couples a great opportunity to be able to discuss feelings, emotions, and concerns, *and* show their spouses how much they really mean to them.

Some of us may not understand how to have a date night. Allow me to give you some examples on how to have a simple, date night and an incredible time with your spouse. The two of you could go to the local drive-in movie theatre, and afterwards stop to get a scoop of ice-cream. The drive-in movie theatre is inexpensive and will save you much more money than going to the regular movie theater, and afterwards, sharing a scoop or two of ice cream. This can be quite relaxing for both of you. Essentially, both the drive-in and ice cream date will give you privacy while you are enjoying your night out, and help rekindle the comfort and sweetness in the time you spend together.

While eating the scoop of ice-cream, the two of you can use that time to have a peaceful and relaxed conversation about your marriage, and be comfortable enough to really open up about how you feel and what's been on your mind. Some might say that they do not have the money to go to the movies or go get ice cream. Perhaps you can have an old-fashioned date where the two of you go to a park, promenade, or beach, with your own snacks, and walk around or find a cozy spot to sit and enjoy each other's company. Perhaps sharing a Big Mac or Double Whopper with heavy onions is your food

NO MORE DYSFUNCTIONAL LOVE

choice. At any rate, and regardless of personal taste, a night alone together is worth going the extra mile. Going downtown and staying overnight in a hotel is a good way to enjoy a complete evening together. Though going out of town for the weekend is an extended date, do not hesitate to take advantage of it if time and resources permit it. Ultimately, spending quality time is extremely important when it comes to marriage.

Before I close out this chapter, I'd like to help the person that has completely forgotten how to be romantic. The term *romantic* is defined as inclining toward or suggestive of the feeling of excitement and mystery associated with love. Men, you can buy her roses or yellow tulips and have the bouquet sent to her job. Maybe a gift card to her favorite clothing store or making a reservation for her at the day spa to allow her to relax and be pampered can also be possible suggestions. Ladies, feel free to use that gift card (or of course, your own resources) to purchase negligee or something else your husband would like to see you in. Also, don't hesitate to purchase items and tokens of appreciation for him, depending on his likes. Tickets to a basketball or football game are good, or even a new gadget from Radio Shack or Home Depot might bring a smile to his face. You know your mate, so tailor-make your romantic gift to fit their interests. I promise if you put all of these actions to work, you will experience a stronger and healthier marriage. Last but certainly not least, a marriage is stronger when you keep God involved, so if you don't have a church home, find one so that you can attend as a family and seek God together. Make sure that this place of worship works for you and your family, meeting all of your spiritual needs. Always take time out of your day to read your bible and pray together, even if only for five or ten minutes. Remember to always love on each other no matter what you are facing. I am Pastor Angelo Swinson and I approve this message.

CHAPTER EIGHT
PUTTING GOD FIRST

"When we put God first, all other things fall into their proper place or drop out of our lives" — **Ezra Taft Benson**

Putting God first is something that all Christian couples should be accustomed to. A lot of us have heard the saying, "Only what you do for Christ will last." When you go with God, you can never go wrong. I would like to break down the true meaning of putting God first and the importance of it. I believe that we must first understand what the word *first* means.

First is defined as coming before all others in time or order; earliest. The scriptures tell us in Proverbs 3:6, "In all your ways acknowledge him, and he will make your paths straight." Whenever you decide to acknowledge God, you are saying, "God I want to put You in control of our lives. We want you to lead, guide, and direct us in all that we do." You will realize that by doing this, you set yourselves up for blessings and protection.

Psalms 91

"Whoever dwells in the shelter of the Most High will rest in the shadow of the Almighty. I will say of the Lord, *'He is my refuge and my fortress, my God, in whom I trust.'"*

Many of us have seen and heard others talk about all they had left was their faith. Someone reading this chapter is saying, "I know about having faith, but do you really understand how times get hard?" Sometimes you may not feel like praying or worshipping.

NO MORE DYSFUNCTIONAL LOVE
Matthew 17:20

"He replied, 'Because you have so little faith. I tell you the truth, if you have faith as small as a mustard seed, you can say to this mountain, "Move from here to there" and it will move. Nothing will be impossible for you.'"

I would like to call this "MSF Syndrome" or "Mustard Seed Faith Syndrome." MSF is something that happens in a series. A *mustard seed* is about 1/20th of an inch in size. It doesn't take much to move God. If you add faith to your daily exercise, you will see your life in a different way. Will your faith be tested at times? Will you feel like you want to give up? Will you feel like what you are facing is bigger than you? God is saying that all you need is a little faith, not much, and He'll take care of the giant that is in your life.

Zechariah 4:6

"So he said to me, "This is the word of the LORD to Zerubbabel: 'Not by might nor by power, but by my Spirit,' says the LORD Almighty."

When you have built up your faith in who God is, it becomes easier to trust in Him.

Now, in order to put God first you have to have *faith*, or complete trust or confidence, in Him. Someone that is reading this chapter is probably wondering how to build up their faith. Spending time with God is the best way to get to know Him and what He is capable of.

Spending time in prayer, in worship, and in His presence will build up your faith in God.

Deuteronomy 31:6

*"Be strong and courageous. Do not be afraid or terrified because of them, for the L*ORD *your God goes with you; he will never leave you nor forsake you."*

God wants to remind you that when you commit yourself to Him, He will be committed to you.

NO MORE DYSFUNCTIONAL LOVE

When you connect with who God is, it makes you want to do better in regards to yourself and other relationships you're in. Whenever you give God your heart, He reveals Himself to you; even more so, He shows you who you are. He'll then reveal what you are supposed to do for those that are around you, and your destiny in Him.

I would like to expound on that topic for a few moments. The closer you get to God, the more *selfless*, or concerned more with the needs and wishes of others than with one's own, you become. Whenever you commit yourself to God, only then will you be able to affectively love not only yourself, but also eventually the one God has for you.

The more you put God first, the more things will begin to fall in place. Michael remembers sometime ago when an Elder at his church ministered a message entitled, "Fail to Plan." Whenever you fail to plan, you plan to fail. In order to make things work, you must make God your first *priority*, or a thing that is regarded as more important than another. Putting God first causes everything else to fall into place and become well balanced.

The importance of putting God first is something that all couples should consider.

Hebrews 11:6

"But without faith it is impossible to please him: for he that cometh to God must believe that he is, and that he is a rewarder of them that diligently seek him."

Diligently is defined as constant in effort to accomplish something. Whenever a couple allows God to be the central focus of their relationship, they set themselves up for the favor of God to reign in their lives. Whenever God is in control, they are guaranteed to succeed. Even when they are faced with challenges, they are able to wholly depend on God.

Psalm 55:22

NO MORE DYSFUNCTIONAL LOVE

"Cast thy burden upon the LORD, and he shall sustain thee: he shall never suffer the righteous to be moved."

This means in everything you do or face, you must trust God.

Proverbs 3:6

"In all thy ways acknowledge him, and he shall direct thy paths." In every aspect, let Him be your focal point."

I would like to introduce you to a couple whom I deeply admire: Michael and Michelle. They have displayed what it means to put God first. They met at a church function one day in West Palm Beach, Florida. Michael decided to attend a service that night at a church where Michelle's father was the pastor. They met at the age of six, and then again at the age of 14. Michelle happened to be doing praise and worship that night, and the anointing in her voice had caught the full attention of Michael, even at his youthful age. This alone made her stand out amongst all of the other young ladies that attended the church. He can remember seeing Michelle have a special glory about her, which completely captivated him.

At that moment, Michael built up enough boldness on the inside to ask Michelle to be his lady-friend. Immediately, Michelle responds by saying she didn't love him! Michael responded confidently, saying, "But, I don't expect you to love me right away, but you will grow to love me." He said that if she gave him a chance, then that would give her the opportunity to see who he really was. After some time passed, Michelle decided to give Michael a chance to see if he was the one for her.

After she accepted his invitation to date, there was a protocol that Michael followed. He asked Michelle's father if it was okay for him to date Michelle. Upon getting the release from Michelle's father, they dated for 14 years. Back in those times, there was a respect that the men had concerning the lady they wanted to court. This established a solid foundation early in their relationship.

I firmly believe the reason why they would take this approach is because they weren't just thinking about having a temporary girlfriend, but rather someone that they could be with, long-term. As it has always been said, "The first impression is always what someone will remember." During their years of dating, Michael and Michelle broke up for a period of three years. They faced difficulties in their relationship like any other couple. Most of the challenges came with Michael not being saved at the time.

They never faced infidelity or any unfaithfulness issues during their marriage. However, the church they attended encouraged her to leave him due to the sins in his life. During that time, Michael turned his life over to the Lord. Things began to change for the better in their covenant. Putting God first has been a priority and has allowed their marriage to be blessed beyond measure.

When Michael gave his life to Christ, they were able to move to a new city and experience a new beginning. Their marriage blossomed and their love escalated to a whole new level. They have become so connected to one another that strangers think they are twins.

There are many blessings and promises that we receive whenever we put God first. Matthew 6:33 tells us, "But seek ye first the kingdom of God, and his righteousness; and all these things shall be added unto you." Whenever we allow ourselves to diligently seek God, we set ourselves up for an overflow of blessings.

Proverbs 16:3

"Commit your <u>work</u> to the Lord, and your plans will be established."

Many of us don't realize the true meaning of putting God first.

NO MORE DYSFUNCTIONAL LOVE

Whenever you put God first you have so much to gain, and nothing to lose. The favor of God is released over your marriage and family when you serve Him wholeheartedly.

Ephesians 6:7

"Serve wholeheartedly, as if you were serving the Lord, not men"

Matthew 22:37

"And he said to him, 'You shall love the Lord your God with all your heart and with all your soul and with all your mind.'"

God says that when you give Him your all, He will give you His best. *Are you willing to commit your marriage and family to Me?* God says, *I will cause your marriage and family to prosper.* It may not always be an easy process and everything may not always be perfect. My wife and I have had challenges and tests that we have faced. One thing we always remembered is this scripture,

Psalms 37:25

"I was young and now I am old, yet I have never seen the righteous forsaken or their children begging bread."

Always remember that without faith, it is impossible to please God. Remember it is your faith that moves Him!

CHAPTER NINE

WHAT ARE THE *SINGLES* SAYING?

"Marriage preparation should begin now".
-Author Unknown

The purpose of this chapter is very precise in the message that it is conveying. In this world, there are many people who are single and are waiting for their soul mate. I have decided to ask a few singles about what it is they are looking for in a mate.

NO MORE DYSFUNCTIONAL LOVE
Habakkuk 2:2

"And the LORD answered me, and said, Write the vision, and make it plain upon tables, so he may run that reads it."

In order for God to truly bless you with the desires of your heart, you have to make it clear to Him what it is you want. You have not because you ask not; be specific with God. You can't just say, "Oh, I just want a man..." No! Tell God what type of man or woman... *Specific* is defined as clearly defined or identified; be decisive about what you want and make it plain!

Matthew 7:7

"Ask, and it shall be given you; seek, and you shall find; knock, and it shall be opened unto you."

In other words, God is saying to make your request be known to Him.

Psalm 145:16

"You open your hand, and satisfy the desire of every living thing."

However, even with your desires, your prayer should always be, "God, don't give me what I want – give me what I need." I have come to the realization that what you want may not always be what you need.

Let us take a deeper look into what the singles have to say; to know what they are looking for, and maybe why they are still single. *Single* means to be only one in number; one only; unique; sole: a single exam; unmarried. My personal perception of being single doesn't necessarily mean that you can't have someone. I believe that some of the singles are wise in their choices, and are not quick to rush into a relationship. Many, however, are single because they are afraid of being hurt again. No matter the situation, I think that it is very important to know what you want from God during the process of waiting.

Being single does not mean that you don't have what God wants; it means you are being prepared for what God has for you. I am not saying that you will be perfect, but if you lack experience in an area, whether it be cooking, employment, education, or communication, ask for it. Wherever you are lacking, your obedience in working on that area before your mate comes is vital.

James 1:5

"If any of you lack wisdom, let him ask of God, that giveth to all men liberally, and upbraideth not; and it shall be given him."

God has given me the anointing through this book to activate the things that have been lying dormant on the inside of you. Singles, God has given you the go-getter's anointing to be able to attain what you are lacking, so that when your mate comes, you will be in *position*, or a place where someone or something is located or has been put, to receive them.

Now, let's take a look at what some of the men have said they are looking for in a mate. *Look* is defined as an action to direct one's gaze toward someone or something, or in a specified direction. Some have stated that they are not looking for just any relationship, but rather commitment. They are looking for someone who will be genuine and long-term, not seasonal; seasonal is based on where you are currently, whereas a commitment is more of a long-term assurance.

Seasonal means of, relating to, or characteristic of a particular season of the year; the phrase, *long-term*, means long-run, relating to or extending over a relatively long time. This defines the difference between being in a relationship versus having a commitment with someone.

Ladies, in essence, the men are in search of a wife, not just a girlfriend. A wife is not someone that you are with for a mere two or three years; she is someone you can plan grow old with and have everlasting memories. A girlfriend is somebody you are with temporarily, without chance of permanency.

Proverbs 18:22

"Whosoever finds a wife finds a good thing, and obtains favor of the LORD."

Men are looking for someone to love them unconditionally – someone who will be open and share with them. In other words, someone who will pull the potential that is lying dormant on the inside of them. Ultimately, they want someone that will cause them to grow closer to God.

As I said before, one of the main attributes of a successful marriage is effective communication. They must be trustworthy and honest with their mate. Other attributes, such as the ability to handle finances and budget properly are desirable. Additionally, having a desire to raise children and build a strong family unit are also good characteristics to possess. Men are saying they would like to have someone who has unconditional love for them; whether doing good or bad, rich or poor – she is still there.

Some of the men are looking for a mate that is hungry for the things of God. They are looking for someone who is compatible with them, spiritually. The term *compatible* is defined as being able to exist or occur together without conflict. Furthermore, in the sense of compatibility, these men want a woman of God that will be supportive of them and their ministry, and understand the call of God that is on their mate's life. Even more so, these men are looking for someone whom they can like and love, *after* church is over.

Some of the ladies have stated that they're believing God for someone who has stability, and share the same level of interest as they do in life. They are looking for someone with morals, intelligence, and experience with family. The person or mate they are believing God for has to be able to respond under pressure. *Pressure* is the continuous physical force exerted on or against an object by something in contact with it. With this in mind, a woman wants a man to respond with and display strength whenever the trials of life come along. She wants a man that is not selfish and will honor her as his woman of God; a man that will provide for their family and sow seeds into the kingdom; someone who has the heart of a giver, like she does – these are all very important traits.

We understand that these characteristics are very important because balance is essential when it comes to relationships. The women also acknowledged that they need someone who can be there for them emotionally when things are not always flowing properly. They want and need someone to be that strength in the relationship for them when they are weak.

Ultimately, a consistent prayer life is imperative when it comes to selecting a mate. One thing I can remember is that when my wife and I were dating, the main thing that kept us together was prayer. It is a spiritual communion with God, and I pray that this chapter has encouraged and empowered you to know what to look for in a mate, and how to prepare yourself for that person.

Psalm 37:4

*"Delight thyself also in the L*ORD*: and he shall give thee the desires of thine heart."*

Balance is defined as an even distribution of weight, enabling someone or something to remain upright and steady. With balance being in place, stability is the final product.

Allow me to introduce you to a couple by the name of Cherry and Brian. Cherry and Brian met while in high school, but didn't connect until later on. They both resided in Los Angeles, California, and were reconnected when Brian came into her work place unexpectedly. At the time, Cherry had five children and Brian had none. They had only

NO MORE DYSFUNCTIONAL LOVE

dated for a year when Cherry began to notice that Brian had some anger issues that needed to be dealt with.

Brian had verbally abusive habits, and Cherry began to really seek the face of God. She realized that God had better for her, and that she didn't want to settle with Brian. He didn't have the desire to grow in God as Cherry did. She too felt as though she deserved better, and decided she would wait until the right one came along.

Cherry wanted the best of what God had for her, and she felt as though she was *compromising*, or make an agreement or a settlement of a dispute that is reached by each side, making concessions. Cherry was waiting on the person God had for her, and had decided that settling was no longer an option, regardless of her emotions and desire to be loved. Cherry was disappointed that Brian wasn't the one, because she really wanted him to be. Later on, Cherry found out that Brian's father had anger issues as well, which affirmed her petitioning him to get the help he needed.

Cherry and Brian didn't make it as a couple, but she decided to forgive him and remain friends. She understood the power of forgiveness, and that the issues he had were a result of seeds that were planted in him when he was young.

A *seed* is a flowering plant's unit of reproduction, capable of developing into another such plant. Brian thought that women were *inferior*, or lower in rank, status, or quality.

Romans 12:3

"For I say, through the grace given to me, to everyone who is among you, not to think of himself more highly than he ought to think, but to think soberly, as God has dealt to each one a measure of faith."

Cherry, and many others, have learned that being single has taught them to be complete in the Lord

NO MORE DYSFUNCTIONAL LOVE

first, then recognize how valuable they are to God and the kingdom.

Some ladies have stated that the man of their dreams has to be able to take *all* of her – the side of her that is imperfect (not perfect; faulty), that shows when she is not moving under the anointing, speaking in tongues, or being spiritual. They want a man that will accept their issues and ask God how he should handle them; one who will see the issues and know how to love and minister to her in a way that would cause her to become more complete. The side that shows when she is not in church, but rather at home, and it's just the two of them.

Other, single ladies have expressed wanting a man that has a heart after God; a man that knows how to worship, and can take his family to the throne – one that possesses the qualities of being the head of the household. They want a man who knows how to set the atmosphere at home and in the church. Some women have stated that they want a man to be the priest that God has called them to be; a man that can properly cover his family and provide for them in any areas needed. Men of God, these ladies want a man who can see when they are hurting, get direction from God on how to mend their hearts, and to grasp an understanding of their feelings. Essentially, they want someone who is able to be a husband and a friend. I can truly state that I married my best friend; we were friends before we fell in love.

There are some who are married but are not connected on a "friend" level. The element of friendship is very important because when the love and the spiritual side are lacking, how can you be friends? Single people must make sure the *motive* (reason for doing something) for marrying this person is right. If you marry them for pleasure or for an anointing, what happens when they are not the anointed person and you cannot be intimate with them? Will your relationship still be able to stand?

NO MORE DYSFUNCTIONAL LOVE

Some of the ladies have also stated that communication is very important. They want a man who knows how to be open and honest with them. They want a man that is respectful and knows how to appreciate the woman that they have; someone who is fully committed to the relationship and will be faithful; someone who is responsible and knows what to do to get the job done for his family.

The ladies want a man that is complete, persistent, down to earth, and has a good spirit about him. Someone who is well-balanced and has a good head on his shoulders; someone who has goals and dreams, with intelligence as a basis; someone who knows what they want out of life and is not afraid to take a risk, would be an ideal attributes for a mate.

There are a lot of things that come into play when you think of the singles and what they need. Notice I used the word *need* and not *want*; again, what we want is not always what we need. As I did the survey on the statistics and needs of singles, I discovered something very peculiar. For example, both genders are basically looking and believing for the same attributes in a mate – the number one thing being that they are saved and have a relationship with God, and that they put God first in everything they do. Whatever you put God first in will last!

Another collective characteristic is the willingness to provide and take care of their family. Faithfulness was a key factor throughout this study. Fundamentally, a great majority of the singles articulated that they wanted a mate to be supportive, and not judgmental.

NO MORE DYSFUNCTIONAL LOVE

Some Say (Poem for Singles)
Angelo M. Swinson

Some say they are single, some say they are alone

Some say they mingle,

some wait for the right one to come along

Some say they are being kept;

That they deserve the best

There are no exceptions

ANGELO M. SWINSON

So let me make some suggestions

Allow God to heal the rejection

So your mate can enjoy the blessings

This is the verse I recommend

Especially for the men

When a man finds a wife he finds a good thing

There's no telling what patience could bring

Now let me talk to the ladies

You deserve someone who will not degrade thee

A virtuous woman is to get the praises

So I come to bring the latest

Of what it requires

To have what your hearts desires

It is created in worship

When the two connect it will be perfect.

ABOUT THE AUTHOR
ANGELO M. SWINSON

Pastor/Prophet Angelo Swinson was born at only 2lbs 2 oz in Charleston SC. He was considered a miracle child and has overcome many obstacles. Prophet Swinson was raised in the admonition of the Lord. He gave his life to the lord at the age of 17 and begin to preaching the gospel every since. Prophet Angelo Swinson has always been a unique

ANGELO M. SWINSON

Man of God in his earlier years God would use him to speak things that the Lord would show him. Prophet Angelo Swinson is an uprising sought after Man of God. Prophet Angelo Swinson walks in the office of the Prophet. Prophet Swinson not only walks in the office of the prophet but he operates in all of the 5 Fold gifts. Many people have been healed, delivered, and set free through this ministry. Many people across the east coast and across the world have experience the true prophetic anointing upon this Man of God. Prophet Angelo has served in many areas in ministry such as deacon, head of the music department and even youth pastor. Pastor Swinson is married to Prophetess Shantel Swinson and they have 3 children: A son Minister Dontario Moore & Twin Girls Angel & Angelique Swinson. Together they Pastor Servants of Love 5Fold Outreach Ministries in Riverdale GA. They are under the covering of Apostle Eddrick & Pastor Faylonta High in Union City GA. They have been featured on Atlanta 57's Atlanta Live and TBN'S Praise the Lord broadcast.

NO MORE DYSFUNCTIONAL LOVE

Prophet Swinson is also a 2012 Black Essence Grammy award nominee. Prophet Swinson desire is to see the people of God activated and walk in Gods divine will for their lives. As he often quotes you are being processed for his glory to flow in your life. Prophet Swinson has an Associates of arts degree and Associates is in business management. No More Dysfunctional Love is his first book. He is currently working on others to be released at a later date.

Made in the USA
Charleston, SC
05 March 2013